MULTIPLE INCOME STREAMS IN INSURANCE

Create Life Long Financial Security

Vanlear Shepherd

ACKNOWLEDGEMENT

I would like to express my gratitude and appreciation to my longtime friend, and business associate, Elijah M. Hendon Jr. who is a graphic designer, owner of EMH Design Llc. and designer of this book.

If you need someone to help you market your business, I highly advise you to contact him.

You can reach him by email: elijah@emhdesign.net or visit his website at emhdesign.net.

Copyright © Vanlear Shepherd 2019.

All rights reserved under International Copyright Law. Contents and or cover may not be reproduced in whole or in part in any form without the express written consent of the author.

Sales Tools may be used and copied without permission of the author.

INTRODUCTION

Money won't create success, the freedom to make it will.
— Nelson Mandela

First of all, congratulations. With this book you now have the opportunity to earn unlimited income, maintain financial security, control your time, and never have to work for anyone ever again.

This book is especially designed for those who now have their insurance license, or are considering to become licensed, and want to work as an independent agent. More importantly, it's designed for the entrepreneur or someone who is entrepreneurial.

This book is geared to give you a series of ideas, strategies, and topics that you can use to decide what areas of the insurance industry you choose to pursue to build your business and make your money.

With so many ways to make money in the insurance industry, the following chapters will endeavor to give you some clarity and avoid the frustrations so many new agents experience in this business. Clarity accounts for approximately 80% of success and happiness. Lack of clarity is probably more responsible for frustration and under achievement than any other single factor. The following chapters will allow you to become clear on various ways to produce income streams selling insurance.

The potential for earning unlimited income rests solely with you, your goals, and your desires.

Contents

Acknowledgment		ii
Introduction		iii
Chapter 1	Selling Life Insurance	3
Chapter 2	Selling Health Insurance	7
Chapter 3	Selling Annuities	11
Chapter 4	Selling Medicare Advantage	15
Chapter 5	Selling The Medicare Supplement	19
Chapter 6	Selling Employee Benefits	23
Chapter 7	The Enroller	27
Chapter 8	Selling to Federal Employees	31
Chapter 9	Selling Property and Casualty Insurance	35
Chapter 10	Build Your Own Agency	39

Section II

Sales Tools	43
Suggested Reading	56
Recommended Resources	57
About The Author	59

ONE

Selling Life Insurance

A genius without a road map will get lost in any country, but an average person with a road map will find their way to any destination

- Brian Tracy

Let's begin by talking about selling Life Insurance. Life insurance to many is an extremely broad topic. There are so many different types. How do you know which types to sell and to who? As a Life Insurance Agent, it is your job to target your prospects. It is your job to be the guide. It is your job to help people decide on the amounts of life insurance needed.

Once you decide who you are going to sell to, you then have to do what's called "Discovery". You need to ask a series of questions to determine the prospect's situation. Will the prospect leave any debts behind? What will be the cost of final expenses? Is there a mortgage to pay off? Does the prospect want to provide an education fund for children? What income needs will the family have? How much insurance does the prospect currently have?

Once you have completely discovered your prospect's situation, you can then recommend a particular life insurance product. I highly recommend that you use a detailed fact finding tool. A fact finding tool will include: Client and spouse funeral costs, estate and administrative expenses, home mortgage(s) balance, debts (car, credit cards, etc.), emergency fund (6-12 months recommended), education costs for children, and child care costs upon the client's or spouse's death.

Term insurance usually is the best product to take care of the above mentioned requirements and needs. However, oftentimes you will come across clients who are familiar with life insurance products such as Universal Life, Index Universal Life, and Whole Life and already know what they want to buy. Your role then is to just guide them through the process.

I have included a Client Profiler in the Sales Tools section that you will find useful. It is especially useful for gathering information to determine life insurance needs for married couples, individuals, and their children.

Oftentimes I ask some Discovery questions on the fly during just normal conversation and am able to make an appointment and subsequently get additional information to sell the life insurance that is needed.

When I first started out in the business, back in the seventies, I would make lists of target markets. One list of names and phone numbers were of hair dressers. I would call and ask for the owner and subsequently make an appointment to give a presentation.

Back then my largest case came from my dentist, who not only bought life insurance, but allowed be to handle all of his insurance needs, such as disability, his group life insurance, and pension plan for himself and his employees.

Remember that you have a natural market. People that you know and people that you do business with. People such as your barber, hair dresser, dentist, doctor, dry cleaner owner, grocer, accountant, lawyer, electrician, roofer, gardener, landscaper, and the list go on and on. And let's not forget friends, family, and the people you work with.

Most people depend solely on the group life insurance that they receive at work and when they retire they then realize their group life insurance terminates. They do have the option to convert their group term insurance to a whole life plan without providing evidence of insurability within 30 days but at that point they are much older and the older you are the more expensive the premium. So why not identify this huge market and make them aware of the future.

For those who are uninsurable through normal underwriting, there are plans called Modified Whole Life. Plans that are guaranteed issue for people age 45 to age 80 for amounts up to $25,000 with limited benefit for the first two years. These plans are also referred to as Graded Death Benefit Plans.

There are 781 Life Insurance Companies in the United States. When you decide on which company to become licensed with, be sure to choose one that doesn't require you to be Captive. As a Captive agent, you are precluded from writing business with any other company. You want to choose a company that allows you to be Independent. A company that allows you to be licensed with as many other companies as needed to accommodate your clients. One of my favorites is American National Insurance Company. Their home office is located in Galveston, Texas. They have received a financial strength rating of A (Excellent) from A.M. Best as well as an insurer credit rating of A (Strong) from S&P. If you want contracting information, you can contact me at Vanlear51@aol.com.

Don't be a secret agent! Be sure to let people know what you do. Make it a point to broadcast your profession to anyone and everyone with pride. You may even consider setting up a web site to give you an on-line presence. And don't forget using social media and business listings.

Having a life insurance license gives you financial freedom with the potential to generate unlimited income.

6 MULTIPLE INCOME STREAMS IN INSURANCE

TWO

Selling Health Insurance

Take the first step in faith. You don't have to see the whole staircase. Just take the first step.
- Martin Luther King Jr.

Selling health insurance doesn't have to be complicated. However, you are going to have to learn all you can about High Deductible Health Plans (HDHP), Health Savings Accounts (HSA's), medical plans, and everything there is to know about the Affordable Healthcare Act. ACA (Affordable Care Act) knowledge is particularly important if you want to work the business market helping business owners or helping individuals secure medical plans. Your role is to help clients by letting them know what's available. Get contracted with companies such as Humana, Blue Cross Blue Shield, and Kaiser Permanente. These companies will provide you with all the marketing materials you need to help you run your business.

While the Tax Cuts and Jobs Act reduced the tax penalty for individuals who don't have health coverage to $0, effective for 2019, employers are still subject to penalties for failing to comply with certain ACA rules. For example, the IRS is currently enforcing "employer shared responsibility payments" (ESRP) penalties against large employers who fail to meet the ACA requirements to offer qualifying health coverage to their full-time employees. For this purpose, large employers are those with 50 or more full-time or full-time equivalent employees. Knowing how to keep employers compliant and able to avoid significant financial liabilities, enables you to be extremely valuable when prospecting business owners.

The ACA added a new disclosure requirement for group health plans, called a "Summary of Benefits and Coverage" (SBC}, that's intended to help employees make apples-to-apples comparison of different benefit plan features, such as deductibles, out-of-pocket maximums and copayments for various benefits and services. SBC's must be provided during open enrollment, upon an employee's initial eligibility for coverage under the plan, or in response to a request from an employee. For 2018, a penalty of $1,128 per participant can apply for the failure to provide an SBC as required.

Most information on understanding the ACA can be found on the internet at healthcare.gov or cms.gov.

Identifying individual and group health clients will always be a viable way to add to your income stream and create lifelong financial security. Insurance commission renewals are one of the oldest and long lasting forms of residual income.

The commissions for health insurance have come down and they do vary from company to company, however, they will still add to your bottom line. Kaiser Permanente is leading the pack on commissions and renewals. My role has always been to give the best service and provide the best plans to my clients regardless of the commission amounts.

POP QUIZ Circle the correct answer. Check if answers are correct at www.insurancecareer.net. Knowledge builds confidence. Confidence builds trust.

How do you determine how much insurance your client needs?

A. Sell insurance based on how much commission you would like to make.
B. Sell insurance insurance based on what you think they can afford.
C. Sell insurance based on a series of questions that determine their situation.
D. Sell insurance based on what you gave your last client.

Are there specific things that could assist you in helping your clients?

A. Ask them about their credit score.
B. Use a fact finding tool.
C. Talk with their friends and neighbors.
D. Don't ask personal questions.

What is your natural market?

A. Everyone you contact that needs insurance.
B. People on the internet that need insurance.
C. People you never met that you have a natural potential to sell insurance to.
D. People that you know and people that you do business with.

What do I need to know in order to sell health insurance?

A. Become familiar with all medical plans, health savings accounts and the Affordable Care Act.
B. Talk with doctors and nurses about the cost of health care insurance.
C. Visit hospitals and speak with human resource about their policies.
D. Learn the leading factors of what cause people to need health insurance.

What is a large employer as it pertains to health insurance?

A. Companies with 1000 employees and above that are full-time.
B. Any fortune 500 company.
C. Any company publicly traded on the Dow Jones, Nasdaq or Pink Sheet.
D. Those with 50 or more full-time or full-time equivalent employees.

How can I sell health insurance once I am licensed?

A. Wait for someone to contact you.
B. Get contracted by all the leading Healthcare companies.
C. You need to wait 6 months before contacting Healthcare companies.
D. You qualify once you earn $25,000 in life insurance commissions.

THREE

Selling Annuities

If you want to be happy, set a goal that commands your thoughts, liberates your energy, and inspires your hopes.
— Andrew Carnegie

When talking to your clients, don't forget to ask them about their retirement plan. Many people are participating in their 401k at their place of employment. However, when it comes time to change jobs or retire, they often look for a place to roll over their 401k or their Thrift Savings Plan (TSP) if they are a Federal Employee.

If you are looking for a target market with 2 million civilian workers, you may want to consider working with federal employees. Thirty-one percent of the federal workforce was eligible to retire in 2017, according to a 2014 projection from the government. In 2017, 96,000 federal employees retired. That makes for an endless source of prospects creating the opportunity to help federal employees roll over their Thrift Savings Plan into a qualifying annuity. This market alone, helping employees with roll-overs, can generate commissions of up to 9 and 10% of the amount being rolled over. Many employees have amassed amounts of up to and over $500,000. With your insurance license and having a clear understanding of fixed annuities, you are in a great position to provide risk-averse clients with a variety of solutions to help them achieve their retirement goals.

Fixed Index Annuities have benefited thousands of contract owners over the last decade, providing them with protection of principal and retention of accumulated interest.

Historically, many FIA's had surrender charge schedules of 10 years or longer. However, today's product design includes FIA's with surrender periods as short as five years. In addition, FIA's offer multiple ways to access funds without penalties. Features such as penalty-free withdrawal provisions, loans, and full accumulation value at death are common.

After learning a few basic terms, as with variable annuities, FIA's are understandable. Most companies offer resources to ensure a full understanding of FIA's in order to make educated financial decisions for clients.

FIA's are fixed products with a primary objective of preserving principal. When the guarantees of FIA's offer are considered, the index interest opportunity will be an appealing combination of protection and potential for your clientele.

FIA's offer multiple ways to access accumulated values without taking annuitization. While some values may be available only through annuitization, most current product designs allow for either lump-sum access or a guaranteed lifetime withdrawal stream similar to living benefits within Variable Annuities.

A fixed index annuity offers a unique combination of benefits that can help your clients achieve their long-term goals. No other product offers the tax deferral, indexed interest potential and optional benefits to protect their retirement assets and income.

A number of years ago, I ran a full page ad in the Delta News Digest. The Delta News Digest is a biweekly publication for the people of Delta Airlines, reaching 80 thousand employees and retirees. The ad described a specific annuity offered by Allianz Life Insurance Company with graphics created by Elijah Hendon of EMH Design.

That ad generated calls from retirees, airline pilots, and all level of employees wanting information on rolling over their 401k. My very first sale came from Cheryl. She saw the ad, gave me a call, and after my presentation decided to roll over $150,000 which generated a commission of $12,500. Fielding those telephone calls was exciting and profitable.

So be sure to take advantage of this very viable income stream and at the same time help your clients experience tax-deferred growth, potential marketing index gains that are locked in, with protection from market loss.

POP QUIZ Circle the correct answer. Check if answers are correct at www.insurancecareer.net. Knowledge builds confidence. Confidence builds trust.

Who would be most interested in buying an Annuity?

A. People with 401K plans.
B. People with Thrift Savings Plans.
C. All of the above
D. None of the above

What is your target market for Thrift Savings Plans?

A. Any employee that's ready to retire over the age of 59 1/2 years old.
B. Federal Employees
C. Employees without any plan in place.
D. Non-federal employees that want to rollover a 401K.

What does FIA stand for?

A. Financial Index Allocator
B. Fiduciary Inversion Asset
C. Fixed Investment Annuity
D. Fixed Index Annuity

14 MULTIPLE INCOME STREAMS IN INSURANCE

FOUR

Selling Medicare Advantage

The things you do for yourself are gone when you are gone, but the things you do for others remain as your legacy
— Kalu Ndukwe Kalu

Medicare has different parts that help cover specific services:

Medicare Part A (Hospital Insurance) – Part A helps cover inpatient care in hospitals, including critical access hospitals, and skilled nursing facilities (not custodial or long term care). It also helps cover hospice care and some home health care. Beneficiaries must meet certain conditions to get these benefits. Most people don't pay a premium for Part A because they or a spouse already paid for it through their payroll taxes while working.

Medicare Part B (Medical Insurance) – Part B helps cover doctors' services and outpatient care. It also covers some other medical services that Part A doesn't cover, such as some of the services of physical and occupational therapists, and some home health care. Part B helps pay for these covered services and supplies when they are medically necessary. Most people pay a monthly premium for Part B.

Medicare Part D (Prescription Drug Coverage) – Medicare prescription drug coverage is available to everyone with Medicare. To get Medicare prescription drug coverage, people must join a plan approved by Medicare that offers Medicare drug coverage. Most people pay a monthly premium for Part D.

Medicare Advantage Plans (also known as Medicare Part C) are private insurance plans that reduce your financial risk by covering copayments, coinsurance and deductibles and often include prescription drug coverage. Many plans provide this protection with low or $0 premium plans. Many plans also offer vision, dental, hearing coverage and gym memberships.

Licensed health insurance sales agents can directly sell Medicare Advantage Plans to individuals if they have contracts with the companies that offer these plans. As an agent, you can work independently to sell Medicare Advantage to eligible recipients. One of my favorite companies is Humana even though they don't operate in every state. However, there are many other insurance companies that you can contract with.

There are 75 million baby boomers that are on the verge of retirement. For the next 20 years, an average of 10,000 people each day reaches age 65.

Now is the time to consider how Medicare Advantage products can help you create an income stream that can boost your bottom line. There's never been a better time to start selling Medicare Advantage. Tens of thousands of people are aging into eligibility every day. Tens of millions of people enrolled in Medicare Advantage last year, and more are on the way. Plus, the Baby Boomer market will peak in 2025, making this one of the most lucrative opportunities Agents will see.

You can earn $536 in commissions for beneficiaries new to Medicare and $268 in commissions for renewing Medicare beneficiaries. In states such as California the commissions are even higher. How much would you earn if you just made two sales per week or 100 Medicare Advantage sales annually? With the right marketing plan, the sky is the limit on your earning potential. As a licensed professional, you have the potential opportunity to sell additional products such as life insurance, fixed annuities, final expense coverage, and other products which can further increase your commissions.

To work in this market, you are going to have to learn all you can about Medicare. Additionally, you'll need to understand all of the rules and regulations regarding the sale of Medicare Advantage, the types of Medicare products, and how to stay compliant while selling Medicare Advantage policies.

Be sure to contract with the carriers that offer Medicare Advantage Plans. These carriers include Aetna, United Healthcare, CIGNA, regional Blue Cross and Blue Shields, and Humana, among others. Visit websites or call each insurer to obtain producer requirements and begin the contracting process. Once you've contracted with the individual carrier, you'll be able to sell its products, including Medicare Supplements, talked about in the next chapter.

Every year insurance agents working in the Medicare field must certify with the carriers they represent to sell their Medicare Advantage Plans and prescription drug plans. This is a vital step in agents becoming "ready to sell!"

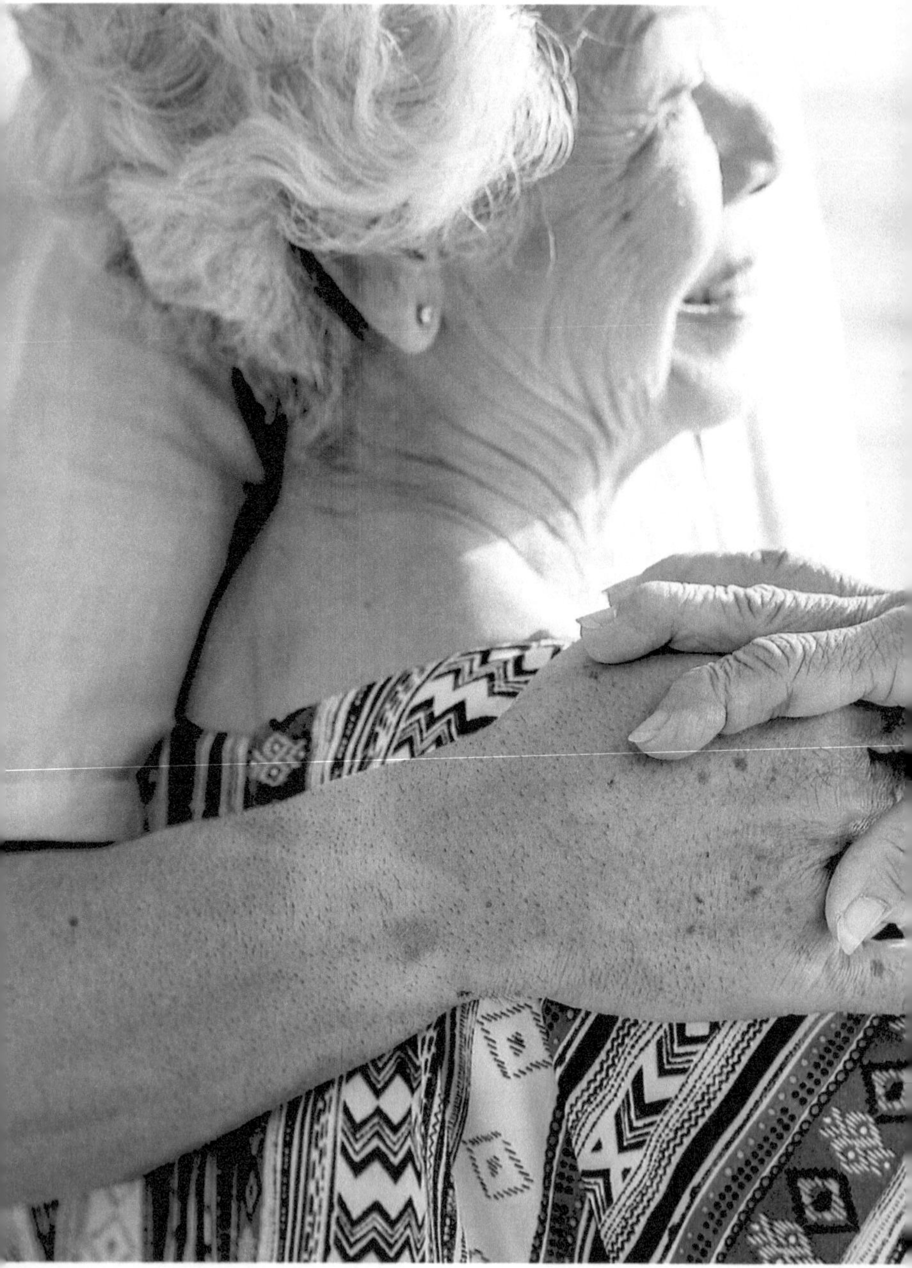

FIVE

Selling The Medicare Supplement

Good, better, best. Never let it rest. Til your good is better and your better is best.

- St. Jerome

The Medicare Supplement is extra health insurance that you buy from a private company to pay health care costs not covered by original Medicare, such as co-payments, co-insurance, deductibles, and health care if you travel outside the United States.

The Medicare Supplement Plan benefits those clients who are chronically ill. Chronically ill patients are those clients that visit the doctor more than three times per month. Generally incurable and ongoing chronic diseases affect approximately 133 million Americans, representing more than 40% of the total population in this country. If you target this market, the commissions can add up quickly, earning you an average commission of around $310 per case.

Chronic diseases include those with arthritis, asthma, cancer, heart disease, diabetes, high blood pressure, cardiovascular illness, Alzheimer's disease, obesity, stroke, alcohol related illnesses, just to name a few illnesses where the Medicare Supplement can benefit your client.

In order to sell Medicare Supplements, a health insurance license is required. Most agents obtain their life and health license at the same time, as they are closely related. In the State of North Carolina, they have a special license that is required as well. In all other states, just a health license is required. You need a non-residence license, easily obtained on line in just minutes, in every state where you intend to sell insurance over the phone or in person.

Medicare Supplements are much simpler to learn, easier to market and sell, and to profit from by helping seniors with their existing plans. Selling Medicare Supplements requires no certification and no company training. It's just like selling a cancer or dental plan.

Medicare Supplements can be sold 365 days per year. There are no restrictions on a specific time frame for selling a Medicare Supplement plan. Unlike Medicare Advantage and Part D drug plans, we get seniors year round who make Medicare Supplement decisions. This can be a lucrative income stream that should not be ignored.

POP QUIZ Circle the correct answer. Check if answers are correct at www.insurancecareer.net. Knowledge builds confidence. Confidence builds trust.

What is a Medicare Advantage plan?

A. Private Insurance plans that cover copayments, coinsurance and deductibles.
B. Government Insurance plans that cover copayments, coinsurance and deductibles.
C. Employer Insurance plans that cover copayments, coinsurance and deductibles.
D. None of the above

On average, how many people reach 60 every day?

A. 1,000 people give or take.
B. 5,000 people give or take.
C. 10,000 people give or take.
D. 100,000 people give or take.

How often do you need certification from the Healthcare providers

A. Once every 5 years.
B. Once every six month.
C. Once every year.
D. Once every 2 years.

What is Medicare Supplement?

A. Extra health insurance from a grant that is not covered by Medicare.
B. Extra health insurance from a your employer that is not covered by Medicare.
C. Extra health insurance from a the government that is not covered by Medicare.
D. Extra health insurance from a private company that is not covered by Medicare.

Who benefits from Medicare Supplements?

A. Anyone who needs medical insurance.
B. Only elderly people 70 or over.
C. People that are ill occassionally.
D. People who are chronically ill.

What is the definition of chronically ill?

A. An illness every other month.
B. An illness once per month.
C. An illness twice per month.
D. An illness three times per month.

What percentage of Americans are affected by chronical illness?

A. Less than 5% of the population.
B. Around 15% of the population..
C. Around 25% of the population.
D. More than 40% of the population.

What types of disease is chronic illness based on?

A. High Blood Pressure.
B. Diabetes.
C. Heart Disease.
D. All of the above.

22 MULTIPLE INCOME STREAMS IN INSURANCE

SIX

Selling Employee Benefits

Strive not to be a success, but rather to be of value.
- Albert Einstein

Approaching corporate clients at first may seem like a daunting task. However, if you are afraid of rejection, don't be. Learn how to handle rejection. Anchor yourself so that the word no, turns you on.

Companies are constantly changing brokers and the insurance products that those brokers bring to them. Get yourself contracted with companies like Unum, Boston Mutual, ING, Humana, and Kaiser. These companies need you to represent them in the market place. They have all of the products, marketing materials, and support you need to make an effective presentation. They need people like you, the sales person, to help increase their profitability and help them stay in business.

One of my favorite companies for voluntary employee benefits is Boston Mutual. Their workplace solutions product portfolio includes Permanent Life Insurance, which is employee paid and guaranteed issued for all eligible employees, Term Life Insurance, Critical Illness Insurance, Accident Insurance, and Disability Insurance, all of which is paid for by the employee through payroll deductions.

As a sales person, you decide who you are going to bring your business to. You decide who gives you the best service in presenting products to the companies you decide to market to.

Now that you have your insurance companies and products in your tool box, the next step is to identify the business you want to approach. This might be the president of the company, the vice president of human resources, the director of human resources, or anyone who might introduce you to one of these contacts. You're going to have to think of creative ways to get yourself in front of one of these people to make yourself known and develop a relationship.

Before an agent can deliver the benefits program an employer wants, he must know what the employer wants. The list of wants can be exhaustive: low cost, high sign-up rate, easy on human resources, the best plans, huge networks, automatic payroll deduction, minimal paperwork, expertly handled eligibility, post-enrollment service and support, easy-to-exchange data, and much more.

One tactic that makes an enrollment easier is to ask company executives and HR folks about the specific objectives of their benefits package. Is the purpose to minimize cost to the employer, shift some of the costs to employees, to encourage wellness, or to have as robust a voluntary suite of products as possible? Often, asking these kinds of questions gets employers thinking of their benefits programs in new ways, and it makes designing or redesigning a program much easier and more beneficial to all involved in the long run. Probing questions are important to help employers achieve the outcomes they want.

Make use of the Employee Benefits Profile fact finder that you will find in the Sales Tools section of this book. The business Snapshot is another tool in the Sales Tools section you can make use of. They are comprehensive and will help you and the client identify areas that may need to be addressed. And finally, after you have secured the deal with the company, use the Business Enrollment Workflow Checklist to keep you on track for a successful enrollment, also located in the Sales Tools section.

It is now time to start developing relationships. Many deals are made on the golf course. Do you belong to the Chamber of Commerce? The Society of Human Resource Management has conventions periodically where the HR people meet who make decisions regarding their employee benefits. For a fee you can set up a booth and make your presence known at these conventions. You can meet and develop relationships with the attendees. Just make sure your business card and company brochures are professional and start to engage the people you come in contact with.

My very first case came from a school board of education in New Jersey. At the time I only offered voluntary permanent life insurance to the employees. Of the 7000 employees, 75% of the total population signed up for the permanent life insurance. Members of the school board, teachers, janitors, cafeteria employees, and bus drivers as well as maintenance workers all participated. The average premium per person was about $520 per year. That case generated close to 3 million dollars in annual premium.

Getting a case this large did require me to hire an enrollment company. Enrollment companies pay the upfront costs of hiring enrollers so the commissions are shared. Nevertheless, I still walked away with a healthy commission.

So it goes without saying, selling employee benefit plans are at the top of my list when it comes to prospecting and should be at the top of your list when looking for a valuable income stream.

SEVEN

The Enroller

Imagination is more important than knowledge
                                    - Albert Einstein

Do you feel like getting away from it all? Do you feel like seeing all parts of the good ole USA? Do you like staying in great hotels, driving great rental cars, having your meals, and travel arrangements all pre-paid, and being paid $200-$300 per day. Then you might like being an Enroller otherwise known as a Benefits Counselor.

Enrollment companies are always looking for licensed individuals to enroll employees in their employee benefit plans. Open enrollment usually takes place from September through December. However, some enrollment companies operate all year round. So if you are free to travel and just want to get away from it all, being an Enroller might be just right for you. If this is something you might want to do, go on line and research enrollment companies.

You'll be responsible for seeing employees face to face with a lap top and enrolling the employees in their medical insurance, group life insurance, dental, vision, and disability insurance, as part of their core benefits. Additionally, you will be required to also enroll employees in their voluntary benefits which include accident plans, critical illness, voluntary permanent life insurance plans, cancer plans, and hospital indemnity plans.

Training usually lasts about two weeks in a classroom and you will be paid for your time. With some companies, you can actually earn $200 to $300 per day plus commission.

If you are new to the insurance industry, being an Enroller will broaden your horizon and give you some in-depth experience in regard to installing employee benefit plans. If you do some research, you can locate enrollment companies all across the country.

Please don't get to comfortable in this JOB. Remember, this is just one idea on the road to getting the feel of the insurance industry. You can use this experience to start your own enrollment company. Use this experience and imagine how you can secure your own case as a Broker and hire an enrollment company to install your own case. Remember you are the one who decides how you are going to make your money while maintaining your financial freedom.

POP QUIZ   Circle the correct answer. Check if answers are correct at www.insurancecareer.net. Knowledge builds confidence. Confidence builds trust.

What is covered under employee benefits?

A. Permanent Life Insurance
B. Disability Insurance
C. Term Life Insurance
D. All of the above

Who do you sell employee benefits to?

A. Company president or owner
B. Human Resource Director
C. Someone who knows the owner or HR director.
D. All of the above

What companies should you contract with to sell employee benefits?

A. Boston Market, Halliburton, U.S. Well Services Inc.
B. Boston Mutual, Humana, ING, Kaiser.
C. ESPN, NBA, E.F. Hutton, Smith Barney.
D. None of the above.

Who do you sell employee benefits to?

A. Company president or owner.
B. Human Resource Director.
C. Someone who knows the owner or HR director.
D. All of the above.

Are there specific things that could assist you in getting an owner or HR director interested?

A. Make small talk and eventually he will ask you.
B. Make your presence known, but wait for him to make the first move.
C. Make use of the Employee Benefits Profile fact finder.
D. None of the above.

What is an enroller?

A. Licensed agents that enroll employees into employee benefits plans
B. Anyone that can sell can be an enroller.
C. There's no such thing, based on insurance laws enrolling is illegal.
D. None of the above.

What can an enroller earn in a day's work?

A. Less than $100 per day.
B. About $150 - $200 per day.
C. Around $200 - $300 per day.
D. Around $350 - $400 per day.

30 MULTIPLE INCOME STREAMS IN INSURANCE

EIGHT

Selling to Federal Employees

It's never crowded along the extra mile
                                        - Wayne Dyer

One very lucrative market is the federal market. Many agents are making sales at the federal employee's worksite. Make sure you understand and follow the policies of the agency. Work closely with managers and supervisors to gain access to federal buildings. Most federal buildings will not allow agents (aka known as advisors) into work areas, but will allow you to set up in break rooms, common areas, and the cafeteria. The facilities manager in federal buildings can be helpful in setting up in common areas. If you are working in a worksite environment, keep your presentation and application session to 15 minutes or less.

Some insurance companies have a Simplified Issue Life Insurance Plan designed for the purpose of selling to federal employees. In most cases, employees can get up to $250,000 of life insurance without a medical exam.

Contact the building facilities manager to schedule days and time you would like to set up a table. They will usually provide one or two tables for you.

The Veterans Administration Hospitals are some of my favorites. You can contact the head of personnel for access.

The following is a list of agencies:

> United States Department of Agriculture
> United States Department of Justice
> United States Department of Commerce
> United States Department of Labor
> United States Department of Defense
> Department of Transportation   Forest Service
> United States Department of Education
> United States Department of the Treasury
> United States Department of Energy   Bureau of the Census
> United States Department of Veterans Affairs   Risk Management Agency
> United States Department of Health and Human Services
> United States Department of Homeland Security
> United States Department of Housing
> Economic Development Administration and Urban Development
> United States Department of the Interior

In the Sales Tools section of this book, you will find a:

Federal Employee Action Sheet. This form is used when setting up a table in one of the Federal Buildings. It's a great tool to use to capture some discovery information, make appointments, and prepare presentations.

Federal Benefit Analysis Client Worksheet. This form is used to capture information on Federal Employees Group Life Insurance. Page two of this worksheet shows the cost of the Federal Employees Group Life Insurance (FEGLI).

Sales Script for Federal Employee Group Life Insurance. This tool can be used when calling federal employees or in just explaining the life insurance costs of the FEGLI compared to private plans.

Sales Script for Pension Maximization. This tool can be used to help federal employees get the most out of their retirement benefits using life insurance.

The Federal Government excluding the Postal Service and soldiers employs about 2 million civilian workers. The Federal Government is the nation's single largest employer. That can be an everlasting income stream.

A few years ago, I contacted the facilities manager at the Federal Building located on Peachtree Street in Atlanta, Georgia. I was allowed to set up two tables for an entire week, providing literature to federal employees presenting various insurance products. I used the above listed Federal Employee Action Sheet to discover what needs employees were interested in and made appointments to see these employees at their workplace. As a result, I was able to sell life insurance, disability insurance, and roll over numerous Thrift Savings Plans into annuities. That one week netted over $20,000.00 in commissions.

Later that month, I set up a table at the Veterans Hospital located in Atlanta, Georgia with similar participation with similar commission results.

There are Veteran Hospitals and federal buildings located in every state of the country more than willing to let you set up information tables in common areas allowing you access to federal employees. So why not take advantage of this under served community of prospects and access this viable income stream.

NINE

Selling Property and Casualty

All the resources we need are in the mind
— Theodore Rooselvelt

For those who have their Property and Casualty License, selling car insurance, homeowners insurance, renters insurance, workman's compensation insurance, commercial property insurance, commercial liability insurance, business owners coverage insurance, and miscellaneous commercial insurance, now have the opportunity for another lucrative income stream.

Everyone that owns and drives a car must have car insurance to drive legally on our roads. Everyone who owns a home is required to have homeowners insurance. People who rent apartments these days are required to purchase renters insurance. Banks require commercial property owners to purchase commercial property insurance in addition to liability insurance. And anyone who owns a business with employees must carry workman's compensation insurance.

The renewals for each of these products provide a constant income stream. Referrals from these clients constantly add to your bottom line each year. Additionally, you will always have the opportunity to cross sell adding additional revenue selling other insurance products.

Let's take Tyler James of Atlanta, Georgia for an example regarding the sale of car insurance.

His main focus since 1998 has always been selling private passenger automobile insurance. He has always worked the Dealership Division of his agency. The Dealership Division is defined as an agent that solicits car dealerships. His days are spent in automobile dealerships speaking with sales people and management. He works dealership hours seven days a week until the phone stops ringing.

Soliciting dealerships has always made sense to him. People go to dealerships to purchase automobiles and he sells automobile insurance. The data shows that 12 percent of the customers that walk into a traditional dealership need automobile insurance. If a dealership caters to a customer base that is high risk, the percentage increases to about 40 percent.

He has always considered the sales personnel at a dealership his clients. He considers his job is to aid the sales person in selling automobiles. That means being available whenever he is called, no matter what time or what day. He is always on call. It enabled him to become part of the sales process and part of the team.

Now if you don't mind being captive, some large companies with their strong multi-media presence will allow you to set up an office in your own community provided you have at least $25,000 in savings. State Farm and Allstate are examples of companies that will set you up in a turnkey office.

Other Property and Casualty agents have opened up their own private office near a Department of Motor Vehicle's office to service customers who need automobile insurance to legally drive.

There are only a few companies in Georgia that will give you an independent contract. They are Progressive, Mercury, Safeco Assurance America, and Infiniti Automobile Insurance Company.

Having your own private office, offers you the opportunity to sell homeowners insurance, life insurance, workman's compensation, and surety bonds, and all the rest. The sales and renewals of these products is another example of multiple income streams.

POP QUIZ Circle the correct answer. Check if answers are correct at www.insurancecareer.net. Knowledge builds confidence. Confidence builds trust.

What is one of many types of insurance you can sell if you have a property and casualty license?

A. Life Insurance
B. Health Insurance
C. Car Insurance
D. All of the above

What is the minimum amount of money it would take to setup a major car insurance agency like Allstate?

A. $20,000
B. $25,000
C. $50,000
D. $100,000

What is a benefit of selling property and casualty insurance?

A. The renewals for each of these products provide a constant income stream.
B. Referrals from these clients constantly add to your bottom line each year.
C. Selling mutiple insurance products to a single client.
D. All of the above.

TEN

Build Your Own Agency

Your imagination is everything. It is the preview of life's coming attraction
                                        - Albert Einstein

With your insurance license you have the opportunity to build your own insurance agency and create lifelong financial security. As long as you are familiar with all of the life and health insurance products, have the right insurance company contracts, have someone who can set you up with the ability to get over rides, have some leadership skills, have some selling and motivational skills, you can build an agency as large as you can imagine.

Being that you fulfilled the requirements to pass the state examination to receive your life and health insurance license, you are already familiar with life and health insurance products. The life and health insurance companies are all to happy to give you all the support you and your agents might need to service your clients. The next step is to find someone or some company to set you up with the ability to receive commissions on the people you recruit in your agency. If you need help in getting the right company contracts and over rides during this phase, I am available for some guidance.

Do you already have leadership skills? If the answer is no. No problem! Just go to your nearest Barnes and Noble booksellers and pick up a few paperback books on leadership skills. And if selling and motivational skills are problem, there are paperbacks for motivational and selling skills too. If you're serious about building an agency, you'll want to have all of your resource material at your fingertips. Make it a point to check the Suggested Reading List in the back of the book.

If you already have the skills we've been talking about, your ability to earn money with your own agency is astronomical. There are many people who would love to have their own business in the insurance industry. You now have that opportunity. The opportunity to create lifelong financial security.

As an agency manager, you have the opportunity to identify, motivate, and train those individuals who want to grow in the insurance industry, improve their life, help other people, and expand their horizons. The more people you help, the better your life will be and the happier you and your family will be.

POP QUIZ Circle the correct answer. Check if answers are correct at www.insurancecareer.net. Knowledge builds confidence. Confidence builds trust.

What is the single most important skill needed to run your own agency?
A. Math Skills
B. Accounting Skills
C. Writing Skills
D. None of the above

If you own an agency, how many agents would you like to have working for you?
A. 3 - 9 agents
B. 10 - 14 agents
C. 15 - 19 agents
D. 20 agents or more

How much would you like to earn, including overrides from your agents?
A. $300,000 yr.
B. $500,000 yr.
C. $700,000 yr.
D. $1,000,000+ yr.

Section II

SALES TOOLS*

1. **Business Snapshot**
1a. **Employee Benefits Profile**
    A tool to use when meeting with a busines owner or someone in charge of employee benefits(decision maker).
2. **Business Enrollment Work flow Checklist**
    A tool to use when installing employee benefits
3. **Employee Sign In Form**
    A tool to keep track of employees
4. **Federal Employee Action Sheet**
    A tool to use when setting up a table in a Federal Building.
5. **Federal Employee Benefit Analysis Client Worksheet**
    A tool to use when sitting with Federal Employees to sell life insurance. Federal employees have 5 year increasing term policies and many have 5 times their salary and are paying to much without realizing it. This is an excellent tool to help employees save money by buying a level term policy or a permanent plan instead.
6. **Sales Script for Federal Employee Group Life Insurance**
7. **Sales Script for Pension Maximization**
8. **Federal Employee Group Life Insurance Costs**
9. **Client Profiler**
    A tool to use when selling individual life insurance

---

* All sales tools are downloadable at www. insurancecareer.net

Business Snapshot

Company Name _____
Business Owner Name(s) _____
Business Contact _____ Phone No. _____
Address _____ Phone No. _____
Email address _____

Business Structure

Sole Proprietor ___ Partnership ___ LLC ___ S-Corp ___ C-Corp ___
We employ ___ Full-time people and ___ seasonal/part-time people.

What's important to me:

Using employee benefits to attract, motivate and retain quality employees? Yes ___ No ___
Offering Medical Insurance? Yes ___ No ___
Voluntary Dental Insurance? Yes ___ No ___
Voluntary Vision Insurance? Yes ___ No ___
Voluntary Disability Insurance? Yes ___ No ___
Voluntary Critical Illness Insurance? Yes ___ No ___
Voluntary Accidental Insurance? Yes ___ No ___
Voluntary Dental Insurance? Yes ___ No ___
Voluntary Individual Life Insurance? Yes ___ No ___
Group Life Insurance? Yes ___ No ___

Business Owner:

Planning for and funding retirement (pension). Yes ___ No ___
Knowing who will get my business should I die. Yes ___ No ___
My family is protected If I die or become disabled. Yes ___ No ___
I currently have a written will. Yes ___ No ___

Securing business life insurance for any of the following:
Key Person Coverage: Yes ___ No ___
Buy-Sell Agreement: Yes ___ No ___

* *Download at www.insurancecareer.net*

1a

Employee Benefits Profile

Company _____ Telephone _____
Address _____
Contact Person _____ # of Employees _____

Current Benefits

Employee Contribution

Group Health	Yes ___ No ___	Yes ___ No ___
Group Life	Yes ___ No ___	Yes ___ No ___
Group Vision	Yes ___ No ___	Yes ___ No ___
Group Dental	Yes ___ No ___	Yes ___ No ___
Group Disability	Yes ___ No ___	Yes ___ No ___
401 (K)	Yes ___ No ___	Yes ___ No ___
Section 125	Yes ___ No ___	Yes ___ No ___
Tax Sheltered Annuity	Yes ___ No ___	Yes ___ No ___
Other _____	Yes ___ No ___	Yes ___ No ___
Other _____	Yes ___ No ___	Yes ___ No ___

Voluntary Payroll Deduction Programs

Employee Contribution

Permanent Life Insurance	Yes ___ No ___	Yes ___ No ___
Disability Insurance	Yes ___ No ___	Yes ___ No ___
Critical Illness Insurance	Yes ___ No ___	Yes ___ No ___
Accidental Insurance	Yes ___ No ___	Yes ___ No ___
Long Term Care Insurance	Yes ___ No ___	Yes ___ No ___
Prepaid Legal Insurance	Yes ___ No ___	Yes ___ No ___
Other _____	Yes ___ No ___	Yes ___ No ___
Other _____	Yes ___ No ___	Yes ___ No ___
Other _____	Yes ___ No ___	Yes ___ No ___

What do you like most about your existing program?
What do your employees like most about your existing program?
What would you change or improve?
What do you think your employees would like to to see changed or improved?
Who, in addition to yourself, would be involved in any decision regarding Employee Benefits?
In general how would you sum up your company's philosophy toward your Employee Benefits Program?

Download at www.insurancecareer.net

Business Enrollment Workflow Checklist

Name of Business _____
Address _____
Phone No. _____ Fax _____ Email address _____
Key Decision Maker _____ Title _____
Personnel Supervisor _____ Title _____
Payroll Supervisor _____ Title _____
Other _____ Title _____

―――――――――――――――――― **Payroll Information** ――――――――――――――――――

Total No. of Employees _____ Payroll Frequency _____ Deduction Frequency _____
First Deduction _____ First Billing Date _____ Date Cards Needed By _____
Billing Order: Alphabetical-Employee No.-SSN-Dept-Other _____

―――――――――――――――――― **Employee Census Data** ――――――――――――――――――

Receive From _____ Date Received _____

―――――――――――― **Department Head Orientation Meeting** ――――――――――――

Scheduled Date _____ Confirmation Date _____ Confirmation By _____ Date _____

―――――――――――――――――― **Annoncement Letters** ――――――――――――――――――

Approved By _____ Date _____ Delivered to _____ Date _____
Scheduled Dist. Date _____ Confirmation Date _____ Confirmation By _____ Date _____

―――――――――――――――――― **Department Heads** ――――――――――――――――――

Name	Title/ Department	Group Meeting Date	Individual Enrollment Date

―――――――――――――――――― **Paperwork** ――――――――――――――――――

Authorization Signed By _____ Date _____
Applications Mailed By _____ Date _____ Case/Tracer No. _____
Emp. Enrollment Reports, Deduction Cards and Waiver Cards Given To _____ Date _____
First Premium Collected $ _____ Date _____ First Billing Reviewed With _____
Arrangements for Employees Not Seen _____
Service Call Frequency _____ Reenrollment Frequency _____
Policy Delivery _____ Miscellaneous _____
Other Considerations _____
Bilingual Enrollers Needed? _____ Security Clearances Needed? _____ Multi-State Locations? _____

Download at www.insurancecareer.net

Employee Sign In Form

Counselor _____   Date _____

#	Name	Phone/Extension	Comments
1.			
2.			
3.			
4.			
5.			
6.			
7.			
8.			
9.			
10.			
11.			
12.			
13.			
14.			
15.			
16.			
17.			
18.			
19.			

Download at www.insurancecareer.net

4

Federal Employee Action Sheet

Name _____

Position _____

Work Number _____ Ext. _____ Cell Number _____

Years of Service _____ Date of Birth _____ Spouse's Date of Birth _____

Marital Status _____

Federal Employee Group Life Insurance

Option A: (Standard $10,000) Yes/No

Option B: Yes / No If yes, how much? 1/ 2/ 3/ 4/ 5 Times (circle one)

Option C: Yes / No

Please check all that applies to your needs and return to Benefits Counselor.

____ Federal Employee Group Life Insurance Analysis

____ Thrift Savings Plan Rollover Information

____ Permanent Life Insurance

____ Pension Maximization Information

____ Long Term Care Insurance

____ Disability Insurance

When do you plan on retiring? _____

Appointment: Date _____ Time _____ Location _____

Download at www.insurancecareer.net

Federal Benefit Analysis

Client Work Sheet

Employee Name _____

Employee Address _____

City _____ State _____ Zip Code _____

Home Phone _____ Cell Phone _____

Employee's Birth Date _____

Spouse's Name _____ Birth Date _____

Federal Employees Group Life Insurance _____

Basic: Yes / No   If Yes, reduction at age 65 (pick one) ____ None _____ 50% ____ 75%

Option A: (Standard $10,000) Yes / No

Option B: Yes / No   If yes, how much?   1 / 2 / 3 / 4 / 5 / Times   Reduce After Age 65? Y / N

Option C: Yes / No   If yes, how much?   1 / 2 / 3 / 4 / 5 / Times   Reduce After Age 65? Y / N

Spouse Covered: Yes / No

Dependents Covered: Yes / No   Current Age _____   Current Age _____

                                                      Current Age _____   Current Age _____

Additional Life Insurance: Yes / No   Policy Type _____   Amount _____

                                                      Policy Type _____   Amount _____

*Download at www.insurancecareer.net

6

Sales Script for Federal Employee Group Life Insurance

Hello, my name is _____ and I am a Benefits Counselor for Federal Employees. My job is to make employees aware of how their life insurance works.

Your Basic Life Insurance is one times your salary and the cost is 15 cents bi-weekly per $1,000 of coverage. This benefit reduces 75% upon retirement.

Your Basic Life Insurance - Option A is a fixed amount of $10,000 of coverage.

Your Basic Life insurance - Option B allows you to elect one, two, three, four, or five times your actual rate of base pay rounded to the next thousand.

If you have Option B, do you know that your Option B Life Insurance goes up every five years and can become extremely expensive and reduces to zero upon retirement?

If you have Option B, do you how much coverage you have and the cost per pay?

There are steps you can take right now to either supplement or replace the ever increasing cost of your Federal Employee Group Life Insurance.

Let me call you ina few days, after you determine how much coverage you have and how much you are paying, and I will give you a quote on permanent plan that will remain level in cost and coverage.

What is your cell phone number and when is the best time to contact you?

Download at www.insurancecareer.net

Sales Script for Pension Maximization

Hello, my name is _____, and I am a Benefits Counselor for Federal Employees. My job is to help employees get the most out of their retirement benefits.

Are you married? (Only proceed if the employee is married)

When you retire, you have the option of choosing one of three retirement benefits. The maximum or the Surviving Spouse Income where your spouse will receive approximately 25% or 50% of your Retirement Income upon death.

Federal employees must at least choose the minimum survivor benefit at retirement in order for their spouse to keep the goverment health insurance if the federal employee predeceases the spouse in retirement.

There is an insurance plan that allows you to take the maximum retirement benefit and still provide for your spouse if you predecease your spouse in retirement.

I would like to show how this plan works to maximize your retirement benefit upon your retirement. Would you be available to meet next Tuesday or Wednesday?

What is your phone number?

Download at www.insurancecareer.net

8

Federal Employees Group Life Insurance Cost

Did you know that your Federal Employee Group Life Insurance (FEGLI) cost increase every 5 years?

Example: Cost of Option B Coverage (at the maximum of 5 times salary) over a 30 year period for a 35 year old Federal Employee earning $50,000 a year.

FEGLI cost is the same for male and female, smoker and non-smoker. Coverage amount is $250,000.

Ages 35 - 39	Bi-weekly Cost =	$	7.50
	Annual Cost =	$	195.00
	5-Year Cost =	$	975.00
Ages 40 - 44	Bi-weekly Cost =	$	12.50
	Annual Cost =	$	325.00
	5-Year Cost =	$	1,625.00
Ages 45 - 49	Bi-weekly Cost =	$	20.50
	Annual Cost =	$	520.00
	5-Year Cost =	$	2,600.00
Ages 50 - 54	Bi-weekly Cost =	$	32.50
	Annual Cost =	$	845.00
	5-Year Cost =	$	4,225.00
Ages 55 - 59	Bi-weekly Cost =	$	57.50
	Annual Cost =	$	1495.00
	5-Year Cost =	$	7,475.00
Ages 60 - 65	Bi-weekly Cost =	$	130.00
	Annual Cost =	$	3,380.00
	5-Year Cost =	$	16,900.00

* Download at www.insurancecareer.net

CLIENT PROFILER

──────────── **Personal Information** ────────────

Client Information

Marital Status: ☐ Single   ☐ Married

First Name _____
Last Name _____
Employement Status:
Employer _____
Position _____
Annual Income _____
Birth Date: _____
Gender: ☐ Male   ☐ Female

Address / Phone:
Line 1 _____
Line 2 _____
City _____
State _____
Zip Code _____
Home Phone _____
Business / Cell Phone _____

Spouse Information

First Name _____
Last Name _____
Employement Status:
Employer _____
Position _____
Annual Income _____
Birth Date: _____
Gender: ☐ Male   ☐ Female

Business / Cell Phone _____

──────────── **Dependents** ────────────

First Name _____
Last Name _____
Birth Date: _____
Gender: ☐ Male   ☐ Female

First Name _____
Last Name _____
Birth Date: _____
Gender: ☐ Male   ☐ Female

First Name _____
Last Name _____
Birth Date: _____
Gender: ☐ Male   ☐ Female

First Name _____
Last Name _____
Birth Date: _____
Gender: ☐ Male   ☐ Female

First Name _____
Last Name _____
Birth Date: _____
Gender: ☐ Male   ☐ Female

First Name _____
Last Name _____
Birth Date: _____
Gender: ☐ Male   ☐ Female

* Download at www.insurancecareer.net

9

CLIENT PROFILER
continued
―――――――― **PROTECTION AND ACCUMULATION INFORMATION** ――――――――

LIFE INSURANCE: Survivor Needs
How important is it to provide financial resources for your dependents, or others in the event of your death?

- ☐ Very Important
- ☐ Moderately Important
- ☐ Neutral
- ☐ Moderately Unimportant
- ☐ Unimportant

Tell me about the life insurance planning that you have done so far.

	Death Benefit	Type of Insurance (WL, Term, Group)	Insurer	Years Acquired
Client	_____	_____	_____	___
	_____	_____	_____	___
Spouse	_____	_____	_____	___
	_____	_____	_____	___
Dependents	_____	_____	_____	___
	_____	_____	_____	___
	_____	_____	_____	___

What do you want your life insurance to do for you and your family.
_____
_____

How did you arrive at the current amount of life insurance that you have?
_____
_____

――――――――――――――――――― **Employment** ―――――――――――――――――――

How important is it to you to replace your earned income in the event you become disabled or suffer a prolonged illness?

- ☐ Very Important
- ☐ Moderately Important
- ☐ Neutral
- ☐ Moderately Unimportant
- ☐ Unimportant

How long could you live on your current assets in the event you become disabled or suffer a prolonged illness?

Client	Spouse
☐ less than 4 weeks	☐ less than 4 weeks
☐ 1-6 months	☐ 1-6 months
☐ 7-12 months	☐ 7-12 months
☐ more than 1 year	☐ more than 1 year

――――――――――――――――――――― **Assets** ―――――――――――――――――――――

Are you currently saving money for any particular goals or objectives (e.g. children's education, retirement, new home, etc.)? _____
_____

Tell me how you are saving money for (children's education, retirement, new home, etc.). How do you feel about your progress so far? _____
_____

* Download at www.insurancecareer.net

Suggested Reading

The Psychology of Selling
By Brian Tracy

The Art of Closing the Sale
By Brian Tracy

Creative Selling
By Ben Feldman

So You Want To Be An Insurance Agent
By Jeff Hastings

The Digital Life Insurance Agent
By Jeff Root

Success
Edited by J.Pincott

Awakened Imagination
By Neville Goddard

Recommended Resources

ExamFX   Insurance Prelicense Training
www.ExamFX.com

The most innovative training available designed to help students pass on the first try is ExamFX. The ExamFX insurance training platform offers a wide variety of prelicensing programs in all 50 states. Each is specifically designed to follow the individual state's testing provider exam online, ensuring that only the information that might be presented in the exam is covered. Use ExamFX to qualify to take your state life and health insurance exam.

Federal Employee Almanac
www.FederalDaily.com

Go to this website to order the edition of the Federal Employees Almanac.
This valuable tool enables you to help federal employees better understand their benefits and helps you to provide the essential products they need to purchase.

Thrift Savings Plan
www.tsp.gov

Go to this website to learn everything there is to know about federal employee's Thrift Savings Plan. Here you will find the forms necessary to roll over their account into a traditional annuity, a indexed annuity, or a immediate annuity.

The American College
www.Theamericancollege.edu

Go to this website to take courses to enhance your insurance knowledge.

Healthcare
www.healthcare.gov
Use this website to learn more about health plans being offered.

Please visit www.insurancecareer.net for updates on the latest trends, new products and information in the insurance industry.

About The Author

Vanlear Shepherd received a Bachelor of Science Degree in Business Administration from Montclair State University located in Upper Montclair, New Jersey in 1975.

He started his insurance career with Metropolitan Life Insurance Company in 1976 where he worked as a Sales Representative for two years before becoming an independent agent representing various insurance companies such as Sun Life of Canada, Mutual of New York, Great American, and John Hancock.

In 1981 he began selling employee benefits and was able to secure one of his largest contracts with a school board consisting of 7000 employees where he was able to secure 75% participation in the voluntary benefits that were offered.

Soon thereafter he took a position with Prudential Insurance Company as a Special Agent selling mutual funds, variable annuities, life insurance as well as health, disability, and long term care insurance for investments and estate planning.

He retired from Prudential at the age of 55. However, he still operates as an independent agent helping large, medium, and small companies enhance their company benefits by offering major medical insurance, various core benefits, as well as voluntary benefits.

He currently resides in the Atlanta Metropolitan area operating an agency helping new agents to become more successful.

www.ingramcontent.com/pod-product-compliance
Lightning Source LLC
Chambersburg PA
CBHW021912170526
45157CB00005B/2057